C000244181

Bygone Kent

**Glyn Kraemer-Johnson
and John Bishop**

Ian Allan
PUBLISHING

Front cover: Folkestone is the setting for East Kent Park Royal-bodied Guy Arab IV GFN 924, bound for Lydd in the late 1950s. Like the bus, Police telephone boxes and cigarette advertising — here asserting that 'Woodbine gives satisfaction' — have long since been consigned to history. *A. P. Tatt*

Previous page: A brand-new BRCW Type 3 diesel-electric, No D6546, trundles through Paddock Wood station with a train of mineral wagons in 1961. At the time such locomotives (later to become known collectively as Class 33) represented the new order on Kent's railway lines, but they are now as much a part of history as the steam engines they replaced. *Marcus Eavis / Online Transport Archive*

Below: Its polished chrome radiator surround gleaming, East Kent Leyland Titan TD5 JG 8229, with lowbridge postwar ECW body, departs Maidstone's Mill Street bus station on the lengthy trunk route to Folkestone, the presence of Maidstone & District AEC Reliances dating the photograph to the late 1950s. Note also the Autovac fuel pump, clearly visible on the nearside front bulkhead. *Martin Llewellyn / Omnicolour*

Introduction

Kentish Man? Or Man of Kent? How do you remember which is which? Quite simple, really: the letters 'KM' (which actually stood for *Kent Messenger*, the local newspaper) adorned the front of nearly every double-decker owned by Maidstone & District, the company that operated in the west of the county. Therefore, a Kentish man is one born west of the River Medway. QED!

Kent is a county of contrasts. It is referred to as the Garden of England because of its many orchards and hop farms. Time was when trainloads of Londoners would arrive in the Kentish towns to spend their two weeks' summer holiday hop-picking — hard work and unpleasant when it was wet but made up for by the drinking and sing-songs in the evenings, the pickers enjoying themselves as only Londoners knew how. Kent is also known as the 'Gateway to Europe', on account of its proximity to France — something from which it has profited by virtue of its ferry terminals and docks, and for which it suffered heavily during World War 2. Much of the Battle of Britain was fought above the fields of Kent.

The Kent Coast resorts of Ramsgate and Margate, the latter with its huge 'Dreamland' funfair, were regular holiday destinations for Londoners during the 1950s, before foreign holidays became the vogue. And, when they did, Kent was at the forefront, offering coach/air services to Paris from Lydd Airport. The East Kent Road Car Co was one of the first operators to offer day trips to the Continent, at one stage loading its coaches onto the huge Seaspeed hovercraft *Princess Anne.*

First published 2009

ISBN 978 0 7110 3390 0

All rights reserved. No part of this book may be reproduced or transmitted in any form or by any means, electronic or mechanical, including photocopying, recording or by any information storage and retrieval system, without permission from the Publisher in writing.

© Ian Allan Publishing 2009

Published by Ian Allan Publishing

an imprint of Ian Allan Publishing Ltd, Hersham, Surrey KT12 4RG
Printed in England by Ian Allan Printing Ltd, Hersham, Surrey KT12 4RG

Code: 0909/B1

Visit the Ian Allan Publishing website at www.ianallanpublishing.com

But it was not all holidays and tourism. Coal mining is not an industry that one would immediately associate with Kent, but there were in fact at least nine collieries in the county, the most famous and longest-lasting being those at Tilmanstone and Betteshanger, which closed in 1986 and 1989 respectively. The collieries gave birth to the East Kent Railway, built to handle coal traffic but later opened to the public. It ceased to operate passenger trains in 1948 and finally closed in the 1980s with the last of the collieries.

Chatham, one of the Medway Towns (the others being Rochester, Strood and Gillingham) was famous for its Naval Dockyard from the time (in the early 16th century) that Henry VIII decided to moor his ships in the Medway. It was from here also that the Medway Steam Packet Co operated its fleet of paddle-steamers on day trips to Sheerness, Ramsgate, Clacton and Southend. One of these was the famous *Medway Queen*, which took part in the Dunkirk evacuation and which is currently undergoing restoration at Chatham Dockyard.

At Rochester was to be found Short Bros, the world's oldest aircraft manufacturer and famous for its Sunderland flying boats. In the 1920s and '30s the company also built bus bodywork, being a regular supplier to local operators East Kent, Maidstone & District and, over the Sussex border, Southdown.

The county town of Maidstone and its environs were home to the Kent's other main industries — primarily paper and flour milling but also motor manufacture. Tilling-Stevens, pioneer of the motor bus, had its factory in Maidstone, and this later became home to the Rootes Group and birthplace of the famous Commer TS3 two-stroke diesel engine. Further west, in Dartford, was the coachbuilder J. C. Beadle. This company was particularly associated with 'chassisless' (integral) construction and made a name for itself in the 1950s by building 'new' coaches using running units from withdrawn prewar vehicles. Later it introduced a range of integral buses and coaches using the aforementioned Commer TS3 engine.

But what of Kent's transport operations? This was as varied as the county itself. In the north-west, red London trams, trolleybuses and motor buses nudged their way as far as Abbey Wood, Sidcup and Dartford, where they rubbed shoulders with green Country Area cousins that in turn could be found as far east as Gravesend and as far south as Tonbridge. Gravesend and Tunbridge Wells were also served by Green Line coaches, which provided a direct service to Central London and beyond.

The competing suburban railway lines from Charing Cross and Cannon Street had been electrified as early as 1926, and by 1939 electrification had spread as far east as Swanley and Maidstone. The main lines to the Kent Coast, however, were to remain steam-worked until 1959, Folkestone and Dover playing host to numerous boat trains, including the famous 'Golden Arrow' and 'Night Ferry'.

The east of the county was as diverse weather-wise as it could be: during the summer months holidaymakers in the coastal resorts would bask in warm sunshine and swim in the sea, while in winter bitter north-easterly winds could bring snow and flooding in devastating proportions. All this was handled quietly and efficiently by the cherry-red and ivory buses of the East Kent Road Car Co. Prewar, East Kent had operated vehicles mainly of Leyland or Dennis manufacture, along with a notable batch of unusual Morris Commercial double-deckers. However, following wartime deliveries of utility Guy Arabs it standardised on the marque for double-deckers until 1958, when it changed its allegiance to AEC, supplier since 1955 of its single-deckers and coaches.

In the western part of the county bus services were operated largely by the dark-green-and-cream vehicles of Maidstone & District, its routes radiating from Maidstone to serve the Medway Towns and west as far as Gravesend and Sevenoaks. To the south they reached Tunbridge Wells and then penetrated Sussex to reach East Grinstead, Hastings and Brighton. M&D did not operate a particularly standardised fleet: Leyland was generally the preferred choice for double-deckers, AEC being favoured for single-deckers and coaches, but this was by no means a hard-and-fast rule; in the 1940s and '50s large numbers of Bristols, double- and single-deck, rumbled past the oasthouses and cherry orchards, while in the early 1960s, having been one of the first customers for Leyland's Atlantean, the company turned to Daimler for the first of three batches of Fleetline double-deckers. M&D also operated trolleybuses following its takeover of Hastings & District, although these perforce confined themselves to Sussex.

To the south-west of the county lies Romney Marsh, a pretty austere and desolate place in winter but home to the Romney, Hythe & Dymchurch Railway. Billed as the world's smallest public railway, this 15in-gauge line was for much of its life more than just the tourist attraction it is today. Children used it regularly to travel to and from school, and during World War 2 it was requisitioned by the War Department and used extensively in the construction of PLUTO (Pipe Line Under The Ocean), built to supply fuel to the Allied forces in northern France following the D-day landings.

Both John and I have strong connections with Kent, and in the photographs that follow we hope to evoke many fond memories of the Garden of England in the decades following World War 2.

Glyn Kraemer-Johnson
Hailsham, East Sussex
July 2009

Where better to begin our photographic journey around Kent than in its county town? One of a trio of Daimler CVG6 models delivered in 1947, Maidstone Corporation No 74 (JKO 638) basks in summer sunshine while on layover at Malling Terrace. That the bodywork was built in the Newcastle area by Northern Coachbuilders, never a common supplier to operators in the South England, is indicative of the need in the lean postwar years to source bus bodies from wherever they could be obtained. The photograph is undated, but the advertisement for Outspan oranges suggests it was taken in the early 1960s. *Martin Llewellyn / Omnicolour*

When, in the late 1920s, Maidstone Corporation withdrew its trams those on the Tovil route were replaced not by trolleybuses (as elsewhere) but directly by motor buses, on account of its lower frequency. Among the first of a new generation of motor buses introduced from 1956 was No 3 (WKP 73), a Massey-bodied Leyland PD2/20 featuring the 'tin front' radiator cowl popularised by Midland Red. Note the delightful split-screen Morris Minor in the background, the 'no waiting' sign' (left) and the absence of yellow lines. *Martin Llewellyn / Omnicolour*

Left: Maidstone's first trolleybuses arrived in 1928, and in 1946/7 the fleet was updated with the delivery of a dozen Sunbeam W models, with bodywork by Northern Coachbuilders. Here No 72 (HKR 11) makes its way along the High Street *en route* to the Fountain Inn, on the A26 road to Tonbridge. Happily this vehicle survives in preservation and nowadays resides at the Trolleybus Museum at Sandtoft, near Doncaster. *John Bishop / Online Transport Archive*

Above: In the early 1960s Maidstone's trolleybus network seemed secure, an extension into Park Wood estate in 1959 being followed by another in 1963. The increased vehicle requirement was met by obtaining trolleybuses second-hand from other trolleybus systems that were closing, notably Hastings and Brighton. Having just crossed the Medway Bridge, No 51 (LCD 51), a Weymann-bodied BUT acquired from Brighton Corporation in 1959, passes the wood yard in Tonbridge Road *en route* to the village of Barming. *John Bishop / Online Transport Archive*

Left: For its motor buses Maidstone continued to standardise on the Massey-bodied Leyland PD2. No 16 (516 RKR), a PD2A/30 model (with distinctive St Helens-style moulded front) dating from 1961, is seen leaving the High Street for Hatherall Road. The date of the picture is unknown, but the flags and bunting outside Westminster Bank suggest a patriotic celebration. *Martin Llewellyn / Omnicolour*

Above: Making a fine sight leaving the Corporation's depot in Tonbridge Road is Maidstone No 20 (20 UKK), a Massey-bodied Leyland PD2A/30 of 1962, still in the municipality's traditional colours of brown and cream. However, close scrutiny of the background reveals the presence of an Atlantean in the later light blue, dating the photograph to between 1965, when this scheme was introduced, and early 1967, when the trolleybus wires came down. *Marcus Eavis / Online Transport Archive*

In the mid-1960s Maidstone Corporation decided to abandon its trolleybus system and in 1965, to commence trolleybus replacement, took delivery of its first Leyland Atlanteans. Showing off the attractive new livery of Fiesta blue and cream which these vehicles introduced, Massey-bodied No 30 (EKP 230C) waits time in the High Street in July 1974. *John Bishop / Online Transport Archive*

Our first visit to Maidstone concludes with this attractive view of Northern Counties-bodied Atlantean 54 (EKR 154L) in Bishop's Way (no relation!) on the one-time trolleybus route to Barming in July 1974. New a year earlier, this was numerically the last vehicle delivered to the Corporation before a radical new policy dictated the purchase of high-capacity lightweight single-deckers. *John Bishop / Online Transport Archive*

Longer-distance services in western Kent were traditionally the responsibility of The Maidstone & District Motor Services. In the spring of 1967 DH388 (NKT 884), one of a large batch of all-Leyland PD2/12 models delivered 1951, calls at Hawkhurst on the long route south from Maidstone to Hastings. Opened in 1950, Hawkhurst bus station, with its distinctive fan-shaped awning, would remain in use until February 2008. *Dave Brown*

Right: A few miles to the north of Hawkhurst is the small country town of Cranbrook, setting for this superb photograph encapsulating so much of bygone Kent. The Policeman's heavy coat contrasts with the floral-patterned dresses as Maidstone & District all-Leyland PD2/12 DH396 (NKT 892) turns into the High Street, passing weather-boarded buildings so typical of the area. *Martin Llewellyn / Omnicolour*

Right: The old market town of Tenterden is noted for historic buildings, not least the 15th-century 'Tudor Rose', which from the late 1920s served as Maidstone & District's enquiry office and behind which was the bus station/garage. Arriving in May 1969 on the cross-country route from Maidstone is Harrington Wayfarer-bodied AEC Reliance 2403 (403 DKK), new in 1958 as a coach but demoted to dual-purpose status in 1965, when a bus-style front was grafted onto its original body. *Martin Llewellyn / Omnicolour*

Tenterden will be known to many transport enthusiasts as being the original terminus of the Kent & East Sussex Railway, which once formed part of Colonel Stephens' empire. Arguably one of his more successful ventures, it ran from Robertsbridge in East Sussex and was later extended to Headcorn, on the main line between Ashford and Tonbridge. Closed in 1961, the original section has reopened progressively since 1974, under the auspices of the Kent & East Sussex Railway Preservation Society; this scene, featuring ex-Army Hunslet 0-6-0 Austerity locomotive No 24 *Rolvenden*, was recorded in August 1980. *John Bishop / Online Transport Archive*

Hugging Kent's southern coastline, famous for the Cinque Ports and for its Martello Towers (built to deter Napoleon's forces from invading from France), is another light railway, this being the 15in-gauge Romney, Hythe & Dymchurch Railway. Running a distance of 13½ miles from Hythe to the old lighthouse (and nuclear power station) at Dungeness, it remains open all year round, fulfilling a social need. The principal intermediate station and the locomotive depot are at New Romney, where this photograph was taken in June 1975 of No 2 *Northern Chief*, a ⅓-scale Gresley Pacific built by Davey, Paxman & Co in 1925. *John Bishop / Online Transport Archive*

Left: Given the popularity of long-distance air travel today it is difficult to realise that in the 1960s even a short hop across the English Channel represented something of an adventure. At Lydd Airport on a dull day in August 1968 a British Air Ferries Bristol Superfreighter, capable of carrying five cars and their passengers, taxies out onto the runway for the short flight to Le Touquet. *Tim Lawrence*

Left: In the early 1970s the motorist heading into Kent along the A259 between Rye and New Romney would be confronted by the sight of retired East Kent buses parked at Coldharbour Farm, near Brenzett. Pictured contemplating its fate in December 1973, EFN 569 was one of a batch of all-Dennis Falcons new in 1950. Happily sister EFN 568 survives today in preservation. *John Bishop*

Right: Along the coast at Folkestone the terrain is very hilly, and in Victorian times this prompted the construction of a number of cliff railways. That at The Leas was built in 1885, the two lines balancing each other on the water principle, and proved so popular that a second pair of lines was added in 1890. Today only one pair remains in use, the other having closed in 1985, but our photograph was taken in the 1950s, when both were still in use and the 'fare' was 2d. *A. P. Tatt*

When train ferries were the normal means of travelling to the Continent 'R1'-class 0-6-0 tank engines were a regular sight heading rakes of Southern carriages over the viaduct at Folkestone Harbour, but March 2009 saw this section of line used for the last time. With calm waters below, a pair of 'R1s' tackle the incline in the late 1950s. *A. P. Tatt*

Following the opening of the Channel Tunnel sea-borne traffic from Folkestone diminished to such an extent that the ferries are now just a memory, but in the late 1950s, when this photograph was taken, it was a very different story. Introduced in 1951 by the SNCF (French Railways), the *Côte d'Azur* remained on the Folkestone service for many years and, being a passenger-only vessel, had very graceful lines. Note railway infrastructure on the quayside, including the signalbox painted in Southern green and cream. *A. P. Tatt*

Whilst open-top buses are readily associated with the Isle of Thanet it is easy to forget that in the early 1970s Folkestone had its own service. Pictured on layover in the bus station in September 1972 is Guy Arab IV/Park Royal GFN 923, new in 1953 and converted to open-top in 1970. Wolverhampton-based Guy Motors, a manufacturer much favoured by East Kent in the early-postwar era, was acquired in 1961 by Jaguar Cars, which itself later became part of the British Leyland conglomeration. *Martin Llewellyn / Omnicolour*

Right: Showing off its graceful lines in this earlier view at Folkestone is HJG 17, a Duple-bodied Dennis Lancet UF coach. Dennis Bros, of Guildford, was another traditional supplier of chassis to East Kent, which took 30 examples of the underfloor-engined Lancet UF. Delivered in 1954, they gave good service, the last not being withdrawn until the early 1970s. *A. P. Tatt*

Right: Duty done. Over the years this field near Seabrook, between Hythe and Folkestone, served as a temporary resting-place for many an ex-East Kent vehicle, that nearest the camera being Leyland Tiger/Park Royal coach JG 9947, dating from 1938. Records indicate that it was last used in 1956 and formally withdrawn the following year, dating the photograph to *c*1957. Note how all traces of the previous owner have been obliterated — a common practice then as now. *A. P. Tatt*

Heading east along the coast from Folkestone we come to the port of Dover. The site of a harbour since Roman times, it expanded massively in the decades following World War 2 to take on the form we know today. This view, recorded on 4 May 1969, features a pair of Sealink ferries — one heading out to sea, the other (right) having recently tied up — and, on the left, with pale-green hull, Townsend's *Free Enterprise II. Howard Butler*

Right: In August 1968 British Rail launched its cross-Channel hovercraft operation, Seaspeed, between Dover and Bolougne, using a pair of SRN4 craft, *Princess Margaret* and *Princess Anne*, of which the former is seen here before entering service. The staff members carrying out servicing work give a good idea of the scale of the craft, which as built measured 130ft in length and 78ft across the beam, and could carry 254 passengers and up to 30 cars; note also that, as on Sealink ferries, the BR 'double-arrow' symbol on the port side is reversed. *Howard Butler*

Right: Another cross-Channel hovercraft operator was Hoverlloyd, which began its Ramsgate–Calais service in 1966 and in 1969 opened its new hoverport — officially Ramsgate International — at Pegwell Bay. In the same year it took delivery of the first of an eventual four SRN4s, of which the *Sir Christopher* (named after Sir Christoper Cockerell, inventor of the hovercraft), was commissioned in 1972. Hoverlloyd and Seaspeed would be merged in the early 1980s to form Hoverspeed, all operations then being transferred to Dover. *John Bishop collection / Online Transport Archive*

Above: A splendid line-up of East Kent buses, recorded at Dover in 1958. From left to right are utility Weymann-bodied Guy Arab BJG 411, Park Royal-bodied Dennis Lancet CFN 132, Leyland TD5/ECW JG 9928, Dennis Lancet CFN 164, lowbridge all-Leyland PD1 CJG 972, Dennis Lancet CFN 166, postwar Guy Arab EFN 182 and finally, unidentifiable, a prewar Leyland Titan and a postwar Guy Arab, both with bodywork by Park Royal. Providing the backdrop is, of course, Dover Castle, which in the half-century since the photograph was taken has seen this area change beyond recognition. *Marcus Eavis / Online Transport Archive*

Right: Dating from 1953, East Kent Guy Arab IV GFN 928 stands in Deal bus station on a dull day in the late 1950s. Its rather tired paintwork does little to detract from the handsome lines of its Park Royal bodywork, which bears a marked resemblance to that produced by the same builder for large numbers London Transport's contemporary RT class of AEC Regents. *A. P. Tatt*

Left: Besides its obvious maritime attractions Ramsgate Harbour held much of interest for the transport enthusiast, this fine view featuring as its centrepiece East Kent CJG 967, an all-Leyland Titan PD1 new in 1948. Close scrutiny of the bus reveals it to be of lowbridge layout with, on the upper deck, four-abreast seating and sunken side gangway, the later protruding into the lower saloon, where it frequently caught out unwary passengers leaving their seats! The photograph was taken in July 1962, by which time the Park Royal-bodied AEC Regent V, represented by the full-front example in the background (left), was establishing itself in the East Kent fleet. *Martin Llewellyn / Omnicolour*

Above: Another view at Ramsgate Harbour in July 1962, this time featuring CFN 121, a 35-seat Park Royal-bodied Dennis Lancet III new to East Kent in 1949 (albeit looking much older). In later life many of this type were rebuilt by enclosing the area over the engine, rendering them suitable for what was then known as one-man operation, but this example remained in substantially original condition; destined to be sold in 1964, it would subsequently be acquired for preservation and, restored to East Kent livery, now looks almost better than it did when new! *Martin Llewellyn / Omnicolour*

Left: A major attraction in Ramsgate — among transport enthusiasts, at least — was the narrow-gauge Ramsgate Tunnel Railway, which utilised much of the alignment of the old Ramsgate Harbour branch (closed 1926) to provided a subterranean link from the harbour to Hereson Road, close to the new main-line station at Dumpton Park. Opened in 1936, it remained in use (save for enforced closure during World War 2, when it was put to use as an air-raid shelter) until 1965, when an accident involving one of the two-car electric trains precipitated its closure. This photograph, taken at Hereson Road in 1959, shows the line in happier times. *A. P. Tatt*

Right: On the occasion of the photographer's visit in July 1974 the old Thanet Tramways depot at St Peter's, Broadstairs, still exuded an air of days gone by, although the vehicles contained therein and awaiting for disposal were now East Kent buses. Fortunately JG 9938, a Leyland Tiger TS8/ Park Royal coach dating from 1937, survived in use as a temporary enquiry office at various locations, ultimately passing into private preservation in 1977. *John Bishop / Online Transport Archive*

Right: Besides having a sizeable allocation of East Kent buses the Isle of Thanet was home to independent Kemp's of Cliftonville, which for many years ran this unique coach. The sole AEC Sabre to be sold in the UK (albeit badged as a Leyland), CBU 636J was new in 1970 to London operator Best's of Ealing, fitted with a new style of ECW coach bodywork (destined to become familiar on Bristol RELH chassis) and a powerful V8 engine. Photographed in August 1978 (in Eastbourne!), it is believed to survive on a farm near Canterbury. *John Bishop / Online Transport Archive*

Left: Circumnavigating the clock tower at the eastern end of the promenade in Margate in August 1962 is PFN 845, one of East Kent's first batch of AEC Regent Vs, delivered in 1958/9 with full-front bodywork by Park Royal. The bright-blue sky implies a fine day, but the rolling waves and the gentleman's heavy overcoat tend to suggest otherwise! *Martin Llewellyn / Omnicolour*

Below left: After the war and before the advent of Continental holidays (which started in earnest in the late 1960s) Britain's seaside resorts were besieged with holidaymakers. Those in Kent were no exception, East Kent Road responding by converting a number of surplus double-deckers to open-top format. So treated in May 1959, Guy Arab/Park Royal BJG 461, dating from 1945, is seen with a good load at Westgate in August 1962.
Martin Llewellyn / Omnicolour

Right: A pair of East Kent Guy Arabs caught by late-afternoon sun at Minnis Bay in August 1962. A lowbridge Park Royal-bodied Mk III model delivered in 1950, EFN 193 is pursued by BJG 472, a Weymann-bodied Mk II new in 1945 and converted to open-top in 1959. Just visible on the extreme right is one of the red enamelled bus-stop flags that were once so typical of East Kent.
Martin Llewellyn / Omnicolour

Left: Seemingly epitomising rural Kent, this idyllic view was in fact recorded in the cathedral city of Canterbury. Its livery of rich crimson and cream complementing its genteel surroundings, an immaculate Park Royal-bodied Guy Arab of East Kent crosses the stream as it enters the city via the West Gate in the early 1960s. *Howard Butler*

Right: A group of children wait for EFN 200, a lowbridge Park Royal-bodied Guy Arab III new to East Kent in 1950, to negotiate Canterbury's West Gate as it heads out of the city on a local service in August 1963. The hanging baskets on the lamp standard are a nice touch. *Martin Llewellyn / Omnicolour*

Following the initial batch of 40 delivered in 1958/9 (see page 30), East Kent's Park Royal-bodied AEC Regent Vs reverted to the traditional half-cab layout and featured a squarer profile. New in 1962, YJG 810 additionally shows off the offside illuminated advertisement popular at the time. Seen approaching Canterbury's West Gate in April 1968, it would serve the company for a further 10 years. *Martin Llewellyn / Omnicolour*

Canterbury was the location of East Kent's head office, as well as a large depot. Providing a contrast in the yard opposite the garage c1957 are MJG 292, a recently delivered dual-purpose AEC Reliance/Beadle, and JG 8714, a Dennis Lancet recovery vehicle. New 20 years earlier, this had had its original Dennis body destroyed by enemy action in 1942, was rebodied by Burlingham the following year and finally, in 1952, received the lorry body seen here, in which form it continued to serve the company until 1958. *A. P. Tatt*

Canterbury bus station was the hub of East Kent's operations. Pictured on 10 October 1963, Park Royal-bodied AEC Regent V WFN 872 waits to head north to Swalecliffe, between Herne Bay and Whitstable, while on the left we see again YJG 810, here showing the forward entrance arrangement of these buses. Note that *Kent Messenger* advertisements were not confined to Maidstone & District vehicles! *John Allpress*

From the bus station we turn our attention to the railway station at Canterbury East, which Class U1 2-6-0 No 31897 is seen departing with a set of three BR Mk 1 carriages in carmine and cream (otherwise known as 'blood and custard'!). The photograph was taken before electrification, in 1958, at which time there was still plenty of goods traffic. *Marcus Eavis / Online Transport Archive*

Above: Leaving Canterbury behind, we head out onto the motorway for this view of a pair of East Kent AEC Reliances, recorded shortly after the motorway's opening in the mid-1960s. New a decade or so previously, MJG 49, with locally built Beadle coachwork, leads a later Park Royal-bodied dual-purpose vehicle *en route* to Manston Aerodrome, on the outskirts of Ramsgate. *Howard Butler*

Right: Just off the old London–Canterbury road, the A2, is the ancient market town and former sea port of Faversham. In terms of bus operators' territories it was also a 'border town', served by both East Kent and Maidstone & District. This splendid photograph from 1959 shows the former's Guy Arab III/Park Royal FFN 385 passing the Guildhall, thrice rebuilt over the years and notable especially for its magnificent clock and tower, added in 1814 following an arson attack by revellers celebrating one of Wellington's victories over Napoleon. *Marcus Eavis / Online Transport Archive*

Left: The view east at Faversham station as an unidentified Maunsell Mogul arrives at the head of an up working in 1959. Note that although the train remains steam-hauled the third rail is in place in readiness for the imminent introduction of new electric multiple-units, some of which can be seen stabled in the distance.
Marcus Eavis / Online Transport Archive

Above: The presence of the conductor rail presages the end of South Eastern steam as 'N'-class Mogul No 31402 pauses at Sittingbourne with a Victoria–Ramsgate working in 1959. Interestingly the train comprises a mix of carmine-and-cream and green stock.
Marcus Eavis / Online Transport Archive

Left: A short distance from the main-line station at Sittingbourne is the southerly terminus of the Sittingbourne & Kemsley Light Railway, a 2ft 6in-gauge line opened in stages from 1877 to link the paper mills of Sittingbourne with Ridham Dock, on the banks of the Swale. However, this traffic was lost in the 1960s, and since 1969 the railway has been run by the Locomotive Club of Great Britain as a tourist line. Having arrived with a train from Sittingbourne, 1924-built Kerr, Stuart 0-4-2T *Melior* is coaled and watered at Kemsley on 30 September 2007. In the background can be seen the industrial pipes which are such a feature of the line. *John Bishop*

Above: For the 2007 and 2008 seasons the majority of services on the Sittingbourne & Kemsley Light Railway were maintained by *Triumph*, a Bagnall 0-6-2T dating from 1934 and here seen at Kemsley Down, where the main sheds are located. At the time of writing a cloud hangs over the line's future, much of the land having been sold to a developer, and it must be hoped that after 40 years in preservation this important relic of Kent's industrial heritage does not succumb to 'progress'. *John Bishop*

Above: On a gloriously sunny day in 1959 'C'-class 0-6-0 No 31495 simmers in the heat while waiting for its passengers to board at Sheerness station. The small '73D' plate on the smokebox door denotes allocation to Gillingham shed.
Marcus Eavis /Online Transport Archive

Right: The same locomotive at Sittingbourne, having arrived with the branch train from Sheerness. Designed by Wainwright for the South Eastern & Chatham Railway and introduced in 1900, the 'C' class numbered more than 100 examples, all but a handful of which survived to pass into BR ownership. Fortunately No 31592, restored to SECR green as No 592, survives on the Bluebell Railway.
Marcus Eavis / Online Transport Archive

Presenting a glorious sight in late-summer sunshine, the paddle-steamer *Medway Queen* sets off across the Thames Estuary from Strood in September 1963, possibly for Southend, destination for many of her excursions at this time. On her funnel can be seen a frame (fitted later in life) from which an 'aft steaming light' might be hoisted the regulatory 15ft higher than the forward light. Built in 1924 by the Ailsa shipyard at Troon, Scotland, she was taken out of service soon after this picture was taken and languished for many years on the River Medina, on the Isle of Wight, but following a few traumas (not least when she sank while some work was being carried out!) the necessary funding has now been secured to permit complete restoration. *Marcus Eavis / Online Transport Archive*

A regular sight off the Kent coast in the 1960s was the General Steam Navigation Co's *Royal Sovereign*, which was used on excursions from London to Sheppey, Margate and Ramsgate, being seen here in 1963 with a full complement of passengers. In 1967 she would be purchased by Townsend Bros, which was seeking to expand its ferry service between Dover to the Continent, and drastically rebuilt as the car-carrying *Autocarrier*, in which guise she would be used until 1973 on the Zeebrugge route. *Marcus Eavis / Online Transport Archive*

Left: In 1955 Maidstone & District absorbed its Chatham & District subsidiary, consolidating its position in the Medway Towns. Among the buses inherited was a batch of Guy Arab IVs new the previous year, which with their lightweight Weymann Orion bodywork and frugal Gardner 6LW engines proved to be economical vehicles. By now officially 5465 (a number it was destined never to carry), DH465 (TKM 359) is seen in Gillingham bus station in June 1968, mere days before withdrawal. *John Bishop / Online Transport Archive*

Below left: Seen in Gillingham bus station on the same dull day in June 1968 day are a pair of contrasting Maidstone & District Leylands. Taking pride of place is DH397 (NKT 893), an all-Leyland PD2/12 new in 1951 (and, as 5397, destined to survive until 1970), while alongside, already bearing its new number, is Atlantean/Metro-Cammell 5501 (501 DKT), new in 1959 as DH501. *John Bishop / Online Transport Archive*

Right: A later, brighter scene in Gillingham bus station, recorded on 29 June 1975 and featuring lowbridge Weymann-bodied Leyland Atlantean 6452 (52 DKT). New in 1959 (as DL52), this was one of a batch which, along with highbridge vehicles bodied by Metro-Cammell, replaced trolleybuses in Hastings. By now in NBC leaf green, it would be withdrawn the following year. *John Bishop / Online Transport Archive*

Left: The Gravesend/Dartford area was once 'pure' Maidstone & District territory, but following the establishment of London Transport the company was obliged to relinquish depots at Dartford and Northfleet, while operating rights in Gravesend were restricted. Delivered earlier in the year, Leyland Atlantean/Metro-Cammell DH513 (513 DKT) heads through Gravesend on a local service in 1959. The cream 'moustache' below the windscreen was a characteristic of rear- and underfloor-engined M&D buses prior to the imposition of NBC's corporate image. *Marcus Eavis / Online Transport Archive*

Above: From 1933 the area to the south and west of Gravesend was served by the green buses of London Transport's Country Bus & Coach Department. Particularly suited to its narrow roads were the ECW-bodied Guy Specials of the GS class; here GS36 (MXX 336), of 1953 vintage, pauses at Longfield before continuing its journey from Gravesend to Hartley Court in May 1967. Scrutiny of the offside reveals an 'NF' plate, denoting allocation to the one-time M&D garage at Northfleet. *John Bishop / Online Transport Archive*

In January 1970 London Transport's Country Area bus and Green Line coach services passed to a newly formed NBC subsidiary, London Country Bus Services Ltd, although the LT influence continued for some time thereafter. Seen in Market Street, Dartford, in May 1974, is London Country SM523 (DPD 523J), a dual-door MCW-bodied AEC Swift delivered three years previously in a lightly modified version of LT's Country Area livery and with full LT-style blind display. *John Bishop / Online Transport Archive*

Among the depots inherited by London Country was the ex-M&D garage at Dartford, while included in its opening fleet of more than 1,200 buses and coaches were around 200 AEC Routemasters. Representing both is this October 1979 view of long-wheelbase RML2452 (JJD 452D), by now repainted in NBC leaf green. As is well known, upon withdrawal by London Country many of this class were reacquired by London Transport for use in Central London; this particular example was to survive thus until 2005, its career in the metropolis coincidentally including a spell working on services contracted to Kentish Bus, successor to London Country in the Dartford area. *John Bishop / Online Transport Archive*

Left: In the mid-1970s London Country suffered chronic vehicle shortages, and to alleviate these it resorted hiring from municipalities such as Bournemouth, Eastbourne and Maidstone. This scene from March 1976 features Eastbourne AEC Regent V/East Lancs 67 (KHC 367) heading through Dartford *en route* to Chelsfield, south of Orpington.
John Bishop / Online Transport Archive

Right: Their livery of light blue and cream standing out on a dismal day, a trio of Maidstone Borough Council Massey-bodied Leyland PD2s huddle together at London Country's Dartford garage in March 1976. The need for such hires is emphasised by the presence (left) of a pair of MCW-bodied AEC Swifts with engines removed.
John Bishop / Online Transport Archive

Right: Hired Eastbourne Regents were also used by Swanley garage, where in March 1976 No 68 (KHC 368) was photographed in company with a pair of AEC Swifts — one apparently disabled, the other (red) on London Transport route 21A from Eltham— and an RF-class AEC Regal IV. These were certainly interesting times for enthusiasts, but one can only wonder what the travelling public must have thought! *John Bishop / Online Transport Archive*

Situated a couple of miles to the west of Dartford, Bexleyheath was traditionally served by the red buses (and trolleybuses) of London Transport and has long formed part of Greater London but qualifies for inclusion in this book by virtue of retaining a Kent postal address. Pictured outside the LT garage (built as trolleybus depot before World War 2, during which it suffered a direct hit) is MD12 (KJD 212P), one of 164 Scania/MCW Metropolitans delivered in 1976/7 following disappointing performances from Leyland products. However, by April 1983, when the photograph was taken, the boot was very much on the other foot, the Metropolitans being replaced (after only seven years) by new Leyland Titans such as T715 (OHV 715Y), partially visible on the right. *John Bishop / Online Transport Archive*

Right: Five years on, and a case of 'all change' at Bexleyheath. Required to tender to retain its routes, London Buses (as successor to London Transport) established a number of semi-autonomous 'low-cost' subsidiaries, among them Bexleybus, which adopted its own fleet-numbering system and a livery akin to that of Eastbourne Buses (which in fact painted quite a number of the vehicles). Pictured outside the garage in March 1988 are Iveco/Robin Hood minibus 67 (D513 FYL), Leyland National 53 (THX 178S) and MCW Metrorider 40 (E640 KYW), while representing the old order is Leyland Titan T849 (A849 SUL), ahead of a Bexleybus Northern Counties-bodied Olympian. Regrettably most of the Bexleyheath-area routes would be lost at the next round of tendering, leading the closure of Bexleybus in 1991, although the garage survives in the ownership of London Central *John Bishop / Online Transport Archive*

Right: Another 'low-cost' London Buses subsidiary was Roundabout, established in 1986 to operate tendered routes in and around Orpington. Pictured in the High Street in March 1988, MCW Metrorider MRL71 (E647 KYW) looks smart in Roundabout's attractive livery of deep red and grey, the overall effect marred only slightly by the none-too-subtle label confirming to intending passengers that this is indeed a BUS. *John Bishop / Online Transport Archive*

Left: Bromley, another London borough to retain a Kent postal address, is the setting for one of London Transport's unloved 'Merlins', in reality 36ft AEC Swifts with MCW bodywork. New in 1968, single-door MB345 (VLW 345G), resting between trips to Eltham in June 1974, would be withdrawn the following year and ultimately exported to Dubai; similar vehicles, often in much-modified form, can still be found in service on the island of Malta. *John Bishop / Online Transport Archive*

Above right: Representing the traditional face of London Transport, AEC Regent III/ Park Royal RT4399 (NXP 753) speeds past a Metro-Cammell-bodied Daimler Fleetline (DMS) at Bromley in June 1974. The 'T' (Leyton) garage code discernible on the nearside is a curiosity and should read 'TB' (Bromley). *John Bishop / Online Transport Archive*

Right: Emphatically not traditional London Transport vehicles were a batch of 20 Ford Transits, with Strachans Pacemaker bodywork, delivered in 1972 for use on new routes that did not justify the use of full-size buses. Pictured at Bromley North station on 6 March 1975, FS10 (MLK 710L) waits depart on the B1 to Eltham. *John Bishop / Online Transport Archive*

Left: In earlier times well known in enthusiast circles on account of its requirement for low-height double-deckers, route 410 (Reigate–Godstone–Bromley) plays host to Northern Counties-bodied Daimler Fleetline AF6 (JPK 106K), one of 11 such vehicles diverted to London Country from Western Welsh in 1972. Wearing the attractive livery adopted by LCBS for its rear-engined double-deckers, the bus is seen in Bromley on 6 March 1975, by which time the road under the offending railway bridge at Oxted had been lowered. *John Bishop / Online Transport Archive*

Above: Kent has many airfields, perhaps the best known being Biggin Hill, which stages an annual air show. On a visit in September 1974 the photographer encountered a number vehicles inherited by London Country from London Transport, including this handsomely proportioned AEC Regal IV, RF548 (NLE548), which, aside from the revised fleetname and the yellow piping around the windows, was in essentially original condition. Alongside and behind can be seen a pair of former Green Line Routemasters — RMC1499 (499 CLT) and RCL2229 (CUV 229C) — demoted to bus work. *John Bishop / Online Transport Archive*

Above: Westerham, south-east of Biggin Hill, was the terminus of a railway branch line from Dunton Green. In this tranquil scene, recorded in 1959, an unidentified locomotive simmers at the head of a push-pull set comprising a pair of Wainwright coaches that had been constructed at Ashford in 1906 as steam railcars and subsequently rebuilt. The empty goods shed suggests a paucity of goods traffic — no doubt a contributory factor in the decision to close the branch in 1961. *Marcus Eavis / Online Transport Archive*

Right: Ex-SECR 'H'-class 0-4-4T No 31239 waits to depart Dunton Green on the short run to Westerham in 1959. Built in 1909 to a Wainwright design, the locomotive was one of a class of 66, all but two of which passed to BR, the majority subsequently being equipped for push-pull working on lines such as this. Happily No 31263 survives in preservation on the Bluebell Railway in neighbouring East Sussex, but any hopes of reopening the Westerham branch were scotched when the trackbed was used for the alignment of part of the M25 motorway. *Marcus Eavis / Online Transport Archive*

Above: As well as being the junction for a railway branch line Dunton Green had its own London Transport bus garage, which in 1970 was inherited by London Country and in this April 1976 view forms the backdrop to the latter's SM535 (DPD 535J), an MCW-bodied AEC Swift delivered in 1971. Note, at the entrance to the garage, the temporary London Transport bus stops and, in the background (right), a one-time Royal Blue Bristol MW6G/ECW coach (744 MDV) hired from Western National to ease the ongoing vehicle shortage. *John Bishop / Online Transport Archive*

Right: Tucked away down a side street, the bus station in Sevenoaks was shared by London Transport (later London Country) and Maidstone & District. Seen on layover in April 1974 is AEC Regal IV/Metro-Cammell RF28 (LYF 379), one of 263 similar vehicles delivered in 1951/2 for Green Line services. At the time of their introduction they were well suited to such work, being fitted with luggage racks and folding doors, and in the 1960s many had their appearance enhanced by the addition of twin headlights and a deep, pale-green waistband, but by the time of this photograph RF28 had been demoted to local bus work. *John Bishop / Online Transport Archive*

Passing typically Kentish weather-boarded buildings and a wonderfully traditional petrol station, Maidstone & District Bristol LL5G/ECW SO53 (MKN 202) heads through Tonbridge in the early 1960s. Much favoured by M&D in the years immediately after World War 2, Bristol chassis (and ECW bodywork) ceased to be available to private-sector operators following nationalisation in 1948, which explains why M&D was still receiving such vehicles as late as 1950. *Martin Llewellyn / Omnicolour*

Rural Kent in all its glory. The cyclist homeward plods his weary way as Maidstone & District AEC Reliance/Weymann S212 (XKT 989) passes through the delightful village of Penshurst, between Tonbridge and Edenbridge, on a circular route from Tunbridge Wells that also took in Chiddingstone and Hever Castle. The bus was one a batch of 12 delivered in 1956/7, these being the first examples of a type to which the company would remain faithful for 10 years. *Martin Llewellyn / Omnicolour*

Left: Running deep into northwest Kent were the apple-green-and-cream buses of Southdown, which reached as far as Gravesend on service 122 (operated jointly with M&D) from Brighton. Pictured in Tonbridge High Street during the summer of 1969, Southdown 791 (RUF 191), a Leyland PD2/12 with handsome East Lancs bodywork, has many miles to go before completing the return journey. *Dave Brown*

Above: Although London Transport buses traditionally ran only as far as Tonbridge, Tunbridge Wells was served by Green Line coaches. This scene, recorded at Tunbridge Wells coach station in June 1973, features comparatively new AEC Reliance/Park Royal RP57 (JPA 157K) loading for the long trek across London to Windsor. Dual-purpose vehicles such as this represented a new image for the Green Line network, having replaced Routemaster double-deckers, but failed to stem the decline in passenger numbers brought about the increasing use of the private motor car; today Tunbridge Wells no longer has a Green Line service, and the coach station too has long since passed into history. *John Bishop / Online Transport Archive*

Above: Local bus services in Tunbridge Wells were, of course, provided by Maidstone & District, represented by this view in Mount Pleasant Road of highbridge all-Leyland PD2/12 DH411 (NKT 907) on route 82; note that the route number is repeated in traditional circled form on the destination blind. At the top of the hill is the cinema, since closed but in 1967, when this photograph was taken, one the town's principal centres of entertainment. *Dave Brown*

Right: An unusual view of similar DH395 (NKT 895), showing to good effect the vehicle's 8ft width and enclosed rear platform. The setting is Church Street in Tunbridge Wells, terminus of route 119 from Brighton and a location little changed since this photograph was taken in the summer of 1967. *Dave Brown*

Above: For many years Tunbridge Wells had two railway stations, Central and West. The former, on the London–Hastings main line, was built by the South Eastern Railway and survives to this day. Tunbridge Wells West, built by the London, Brighton & South Coast Railway, was used by trains from Brighton, as well as from Oxted and from East Grinstead. Here 'H'-class 0-4-4T No 31518, already 50 years old when photographed, arrives from Oxted with a grimy set of Maunsell stock. *Marcus Eavis / Online Transport Archive*

Right: Following closure in the 1980s of the line to Groombridge (the continuation thence to East Grinstead have succumbed in 1967) Tunbridge Wells West was declared redundant, the station building subsequently being taken over by a supermarket. However, the platform and locomotive shed survive and are now used by the Spa Valley Railway, which since 1996 has reopened the Tunbridge Wells–Groombridge section as a preserved line and in 2009 hopes to reconnect with the Uckfield–Oxted line at Eridge. Providing a reminder of the scene half a century ago is this view of the shed, featuring 'H'-class 0-4-4T No 31522 and an unidentified BR Standard 2-6-4 tank. *Marcus Eavis / Online Transport Archive*

Paddock Wood, on the Victoria–Dover main line, was the junction for the Maidstone and Hawkhurst branch lines. This attractive scene, captured in 1961, features ex-South Eastern & Chatham 'C'-class 0-6-0 No 31716, dating from 1901, coupled to a two-car Maunsell carriage set and, curiously, a couple of vans. By now the conductor rail had been installed, and, indeed, a new electric unit can be seen standing at the far platform. Today the Hawkhurst branch is long gone, but trains still work through to Maidstone.
Marcus Eavis / Online Transport Archive

A little to the west of Maidstone, on the line from Paddock Wood, is Wateringbury, location of this splendid SECR station. From the photograph it would seem that the BR station nameboard was about to be discarded; how collectors would value such an item today! Thankfully the building, now Grade II listed, survives, albeit in a state of disrepair. *Marcus Eavis / Online Transport Archive*

Above: In 1960 Maidstone & District took delivery of a batch of 15 Albion Nimbuses with 30-seat bodywork by Harrington. Their compact size made them ideal for lightly used rural routes; here SO309 (309 LKK) waits in the village of West Malling, west of Maidstone, before making the short trip to Mereworth. *Martin Llewellyn / Omnicolour*

Right: Ready to depart for West Malling, Maidstone & District DL22 (LKT 983), a Bristol K6A with wonderfully curvaceous lowbridge bodywork by Weymann, waits time at Bearsted on a bright sunny day in the early 1960s. By now oasthouses were already becoming redundant, that on the left seemingly a prime candidate for conversion to housing. *Martin Llewellyn / Omnicolour*

We complete our tour of Kent where we began, at Maidstone. Pictured crossing the River Medway by means of Maidstone Bridge (designed by none other than Sir Joseph Bazalgette, of Tower Bridge fame) is a Maidstone & District Beadle-AEC, C354 (WKM 354). The first of a batch of 23 such coaches received in 1955/6, this was in fact a rebuild incorporating the running units of an AEC Regal III chassis that had been new in 1949 with prewar Harrington coachwork. In rebuilt form it would serve the company for a further nine years, this view dating from the early 1960s. In apparent defiance of the 'no waiting' sign, the motorcycle sidecar is parked on the pavement! *Martin Llewellyn / Omnicolour*

Pictured about to depart Maidstone's Lower Stone Street bus station in the early 1960s is a Maidstone & District Bristol K6A, No DH111 (HKE 212). Delivered in 1944, it had its original Park Royal utility body replaced in 1951 by the rather more attractive Weymann version seen here, its M&D career being thus extended to 1965. In the background can be seen a lowbridge example of the same body style. *Martin Llewellyn / Omnicolour*

Above: Our backward glance at Kent concludes with a rear view of a Maidstone Corporation trolleybus. Heading for the Bull Inn at Barming, on a route which, once extended from the Fountain Inn, took trolleybuses well beyond the then town boundary, Northern Coachbuilders-bodied Sunbeam W No 65 (HKR 4) glides silently away into the glorious countryside that makes up so much of this fine county. *E. C. Bennett / Online Transport Archive*

Back cover: Photographed in Tunbridge Wells in April 1988, Maidstone & District Bristol VRT/ECW 5807 (PKE 807M) rests between journeys to and from Tonbridge. One of the first National Bus Company subsidiaries to be privatised, in November 1986, M&D initially retained NBC leaf-green livery, although the white waistband gradually gave way to cream, yet to be applied to this bus. Note, however, the new 'M&D' logo that has replaced the NBC arrow symbol; also the legend applied beneath the fleetname to mark the company's 75th anniversary, celebrated in 1986.
John Bishop / Online Transport Archive